OUT OF THIS WORLD

ASTRONAUTS

MARY ELIZABETH SALZMANN

Consulting Editor, Diane Craig, M.A./Reading Specialist

Super Sandcastle

An Imprint of Abdo Publishing
abdopublishing.com

ABDOPUBLISHING.COM

Published by Abdo Publishing, a division of ABDO, PO Box 398166, Minneapolis, Minnesota 55439.

Printed in the United States of America, North Mankato, Minnesota
062015
092015

THIS BOOK CONTAINS RECYCLED MATERIALS

Editor: Alex Kuskowski
Content Developer: Nancy Tuminelly
Cover and Interior Design and Production: Mighty Media, Inc.
Photo Credits: Shutterstock, NASA

Library of Congress Cataloging-in-Publication Data
Salzmann, Mary Elizabeth, 1968- author.
Astronauts / Mary Elizabeth Salzmann ; consulting editor, Diane Craig, M.A./Reading Specialist.
pages cm. -- (Out of this world)
Audience: K to grade 4
ISBN 978-1-62403-742-9
1. Astronauts--Juvenile literature. 2. Astronautics--Juvenile literature. 3. Outer space--Exploration--Juvenile literature. I. Title.
TL793.S194 2016
629.45--dc23
2015002057

Super SandCastle™ books are created by a team of professional educators, reading specialists, and content developers around five essential components—phonemic awareness, phonics, vocabulary, text comprehension, and fluency—to assist young readers as they develop reading skills and strategies and increase their general knowledge. All books are written, reviewed, and leveled for guided reading, early reading intervention, and Accelerated Reader™ programs for use in shared, guided, and independent reading and writing activities to support a balanced approach to literacy instruction.

CONTENTS

ASTRONAUTS

ASTRONAUTS are trained to go into space. That's their job. The first astronauts went into space in 1961. A trip into space is a mission or an expedition.

ASTRONAUT JOBS

Several astronauts go on each mission. They each have special responsibilities.

A **COMMANDER** is the ship's captain. The commander knows about everything that happens on the spacecraft.

MISSION SPECIALISTS do many different things. They take care of the **plumbing** and air conditioning. They organize meals. They go on space walks.

A **FLIGHT ENGINEER** is like a mission specialist. A flight engineer can also help fly the spacecraft.

A **PILOT** controls and operates the spacecraft.

PAYLOAD SPECIALIST

Being an astronaut is not a payload specialist's main job. They go on missions to do experiments. Then they return to their regular jobs.

BECOMING AN ASTRONAUT

FLYING

Astronauts learn to fly jet airplanes. They have to keep practicing. Commanders and **pilots** fly jets for 15 hours each month. Non-pilot astronauts fly jets at least 4 hours each month.

EDUCATION

Astronauts study science and math in college. Then they need at least three years of work experience.

PHYSICAL REQUIREMENTS

ASTRONAUTS MUST PASS HEALTH AND FITNESS TESTS.

ASTRONAUTS must be able to swim and SCUBA dive.

ASTRONAUTS must have excellent eyesight.

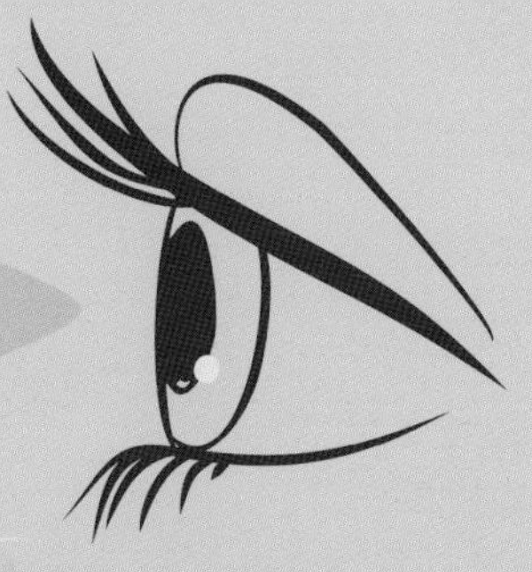

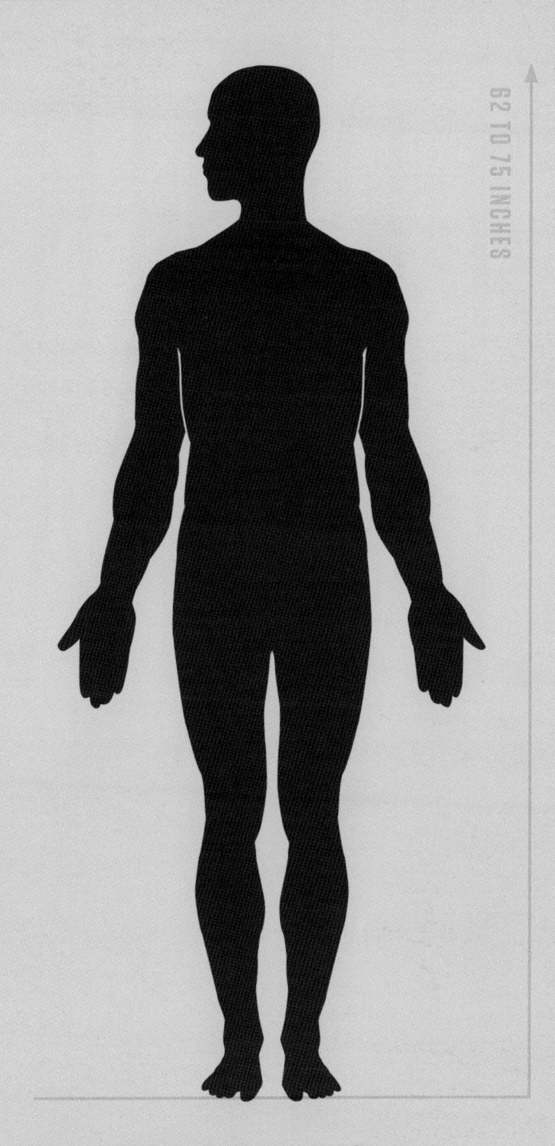

ASTRONAUTS must be 62 to 75 inches (157.5 to 190.5 cm) tall.

LIVING IN SPACE

BEING IN SPACE IS STRANGE. There is no gravity. That means things float around. The astronauts float too!

ON THE INTERNATIONAL SPACE STATION, water is recycled. Breathing and sweating **release** water into the air. It is collected and **filtered**. Then astronauts use it for washing and drinking.

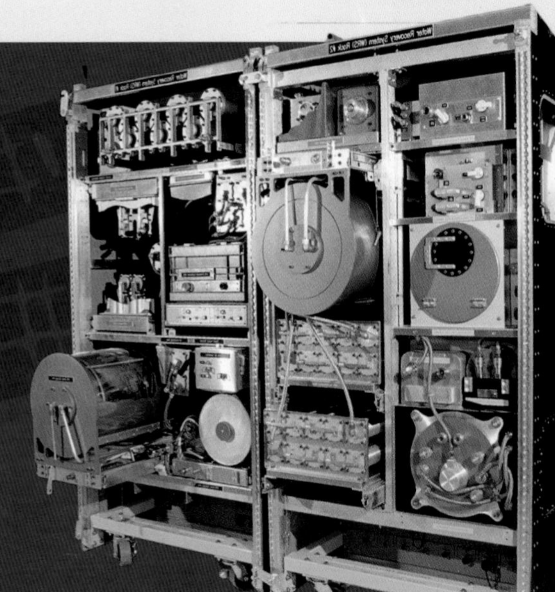

EATING IN SPACE

It is important for astronauts to eat healthy foods. They eat the same foods as they eat on Earth. They eat fruits and vegetables. They eat meat and bread. They drink water, juice, tea, and coffee.

Some foods are easy to eat in space. Other foods are hard to eat in space. An astronaut can easily hold and eat an apple.

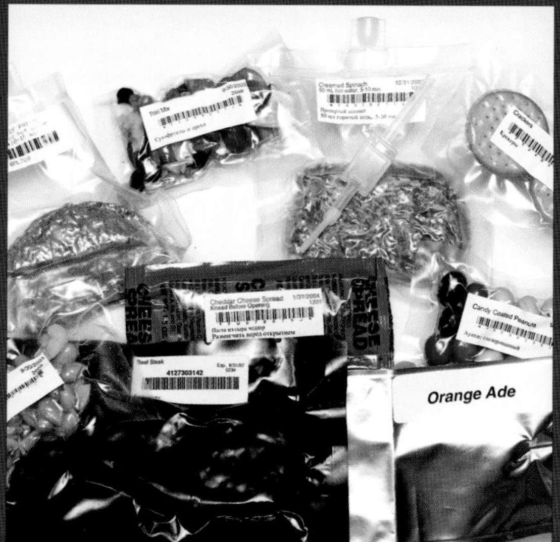

It's harder to eat meals such as spaghetti. They would float right off the plates! So they are wrapped in special packaging.

Drinks come in pouches. The astronauts use straws to drink out of them.

SLEEPING

ASTRONAUTS NEED SLEEP JUST LIKE YOU!

ASTRONAUTS sleep in sleeping bags. They **attach** the sleeping bags to the wall. Then they zip themselves inside.

IN SPACE

AN ASTRONAUT can't sleep in a regular bed. It would float around the room. The astronaut could float right off of the **mattress**!

ASTRONAUT FUN

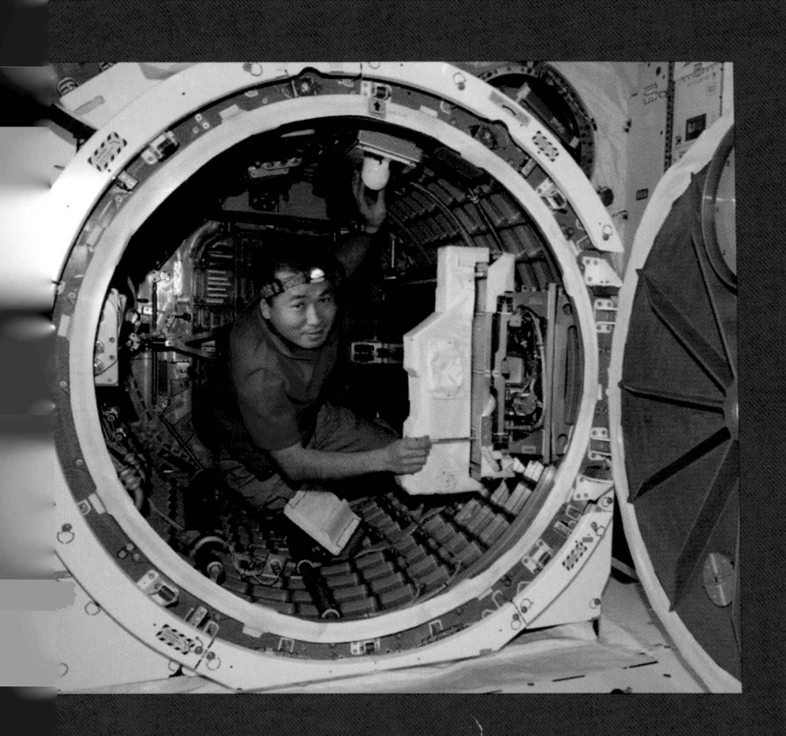

Astronauts don't have to work all the time. They get time off. They can relax and have fun. Astronauts read books, watch movies, and play games. They can talk to friends on Earth.

Astronauts also like to look out the windows. They can see the Earth and other planets. They can see stars and asteroids. There are many cool things to see in space.

STAYING STRONG IN SPACE

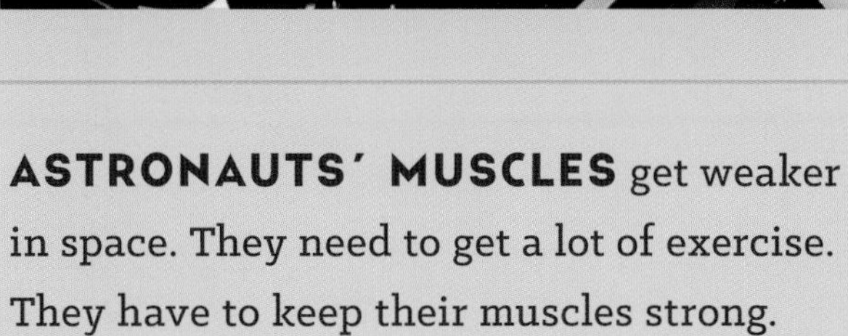

ASTRONAUTS' MUSCLES get weaker in space. They need to get a lot of exercise. They have to keep their muscles strong.

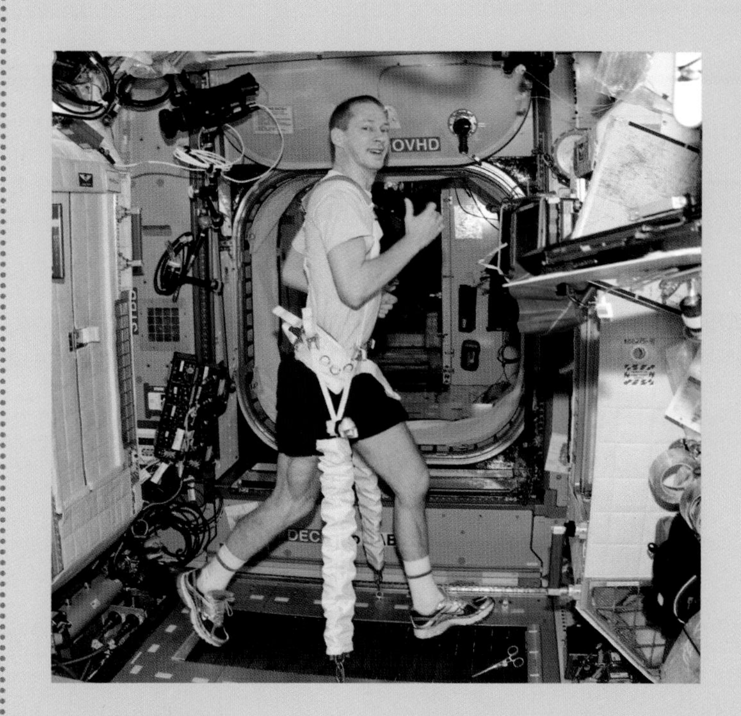

ASTRONAUTS HAVE EXERCISE MACHINES in space. They have treadmills and exercise bikes. Astronauts use them at least 2 hours every day.

SPACE WALK

SOMETIMES ASTRONAUTS LEAVE THE SPACECRAFT.

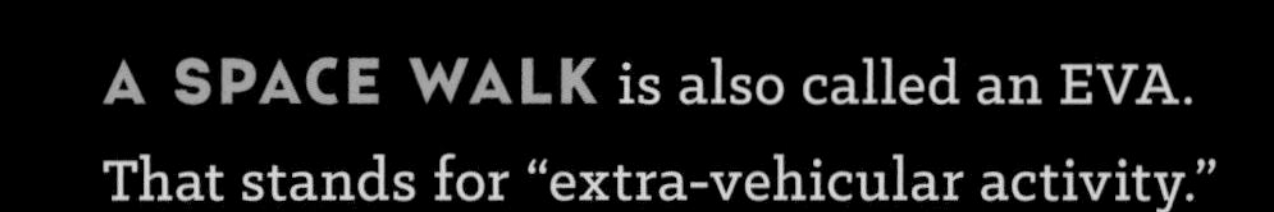

A SPACE WALK is also called an EVA. That stands for "extra-vehicular activity."

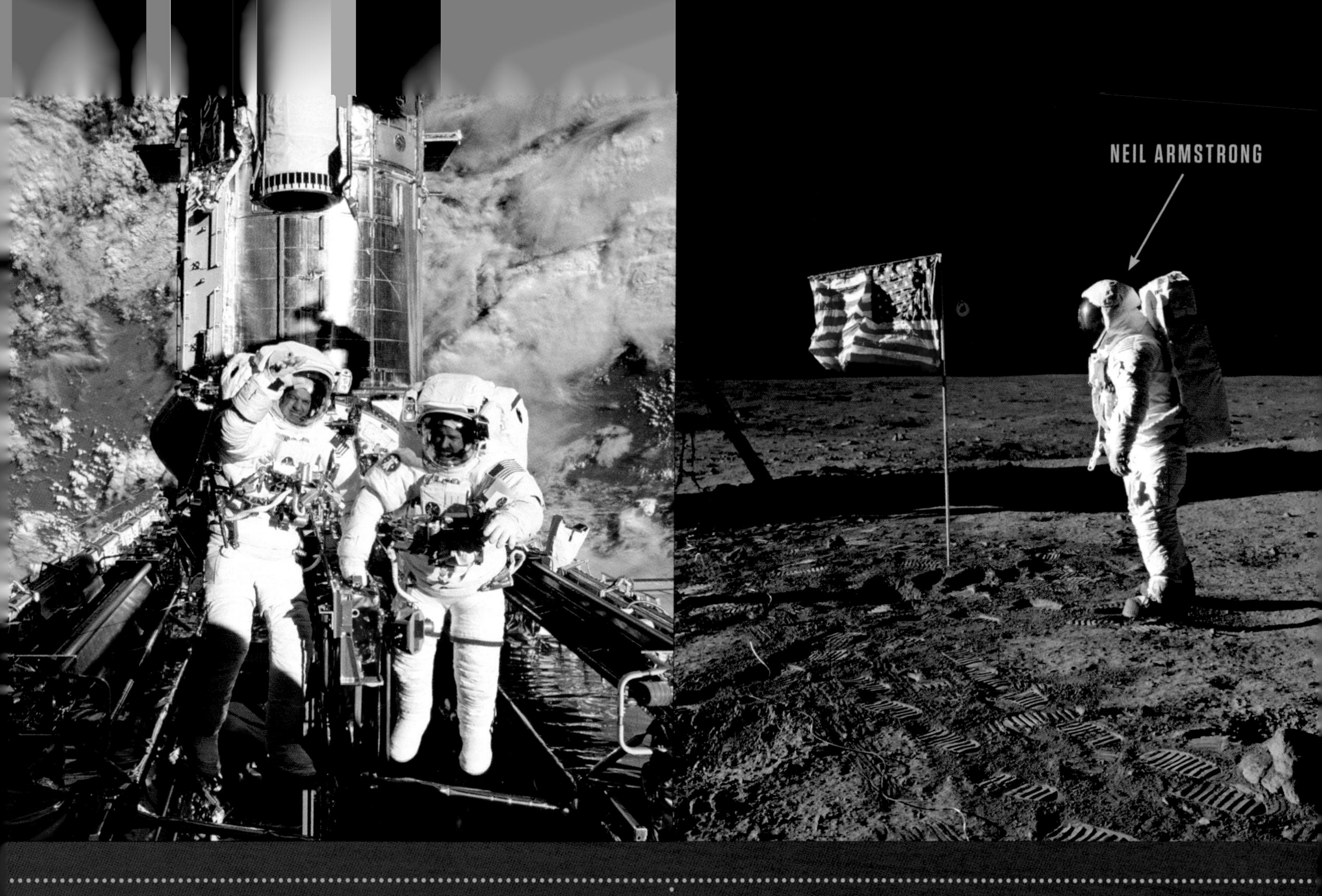

THEY MAKE REPAIRS

They **attach** new parts or **equipment** too.

THEY EXPLORE

They go for a walk on the moon!

SPACE SUIT

AN ASTRONAUT wears a space suit on a space walk.

Oxygen is pumped into the suit. Without it, the astronaut couldn't breathe. That's because there is no oxygen in space.

Space is very cold. It is minus 450 **degrees** Fahrenheit (–270°C)! The space suit has 14 layers to protect the astronaut from the cold.

WHAT IS ON A SPACE SUIT?

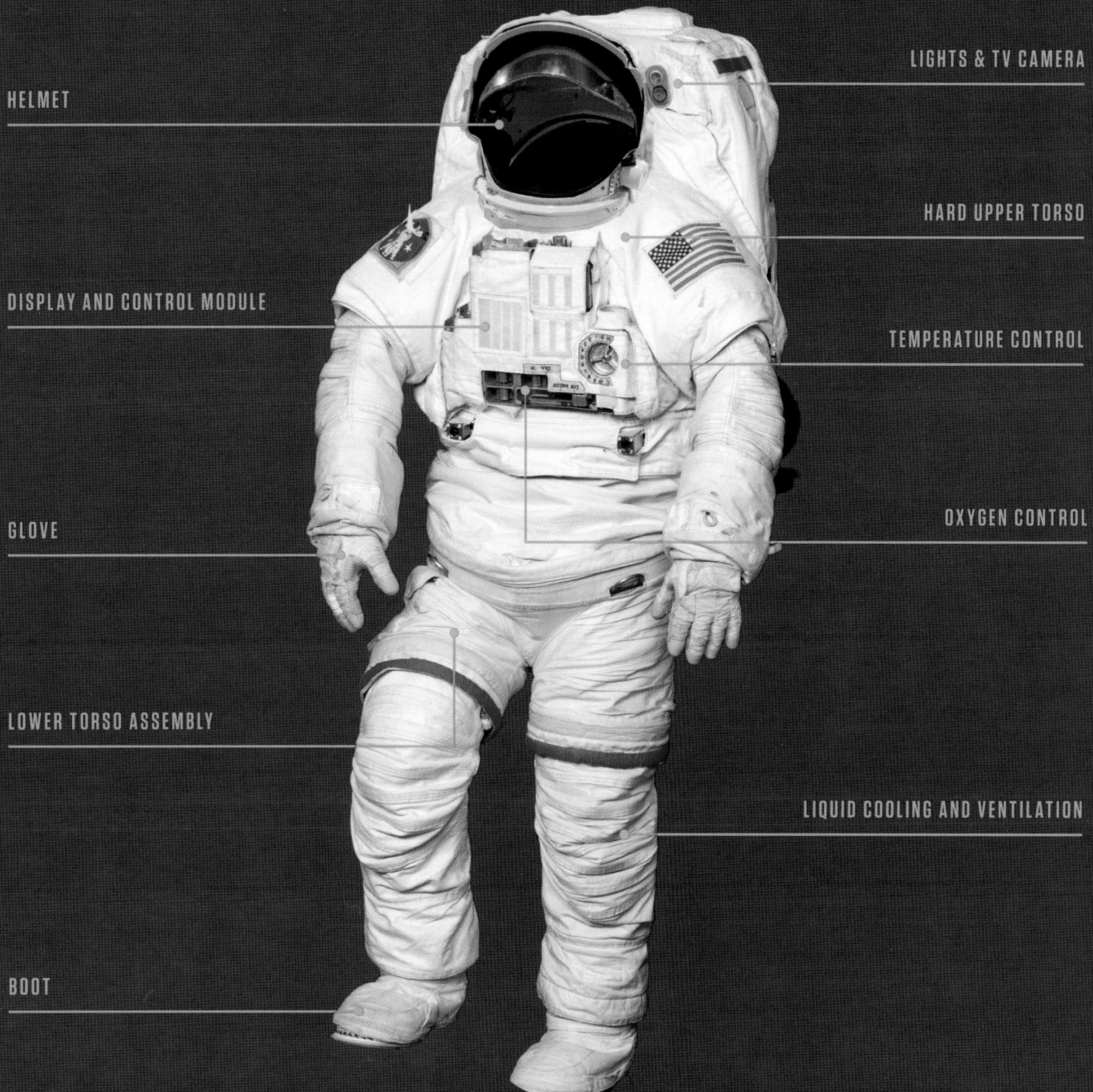

HELMET

LIGHTS & TV CAMERA

HARD UPPER TORSO

DISPLAY AND CONTROL MODULE

TEMPERATURE CONTROL

OXYGEN CONTROL

GLOVE

LOWER TORSO ASSEMBLY

LIQUID COOLING AND VENTILATION

BOOT

SPACE DISASTERS

SPACE SHUTTLE CHALLENGER

The first was the space shuttle *Challenger*. It exploded right after **launching**. It happened on January 28, 1986. All seven crew members died.

BEING AN ASTRONAUT can be **dangerous**. Eighteen astronauts have died while flying space missions. The two worst **disasters** happened when space shuttles exploded.

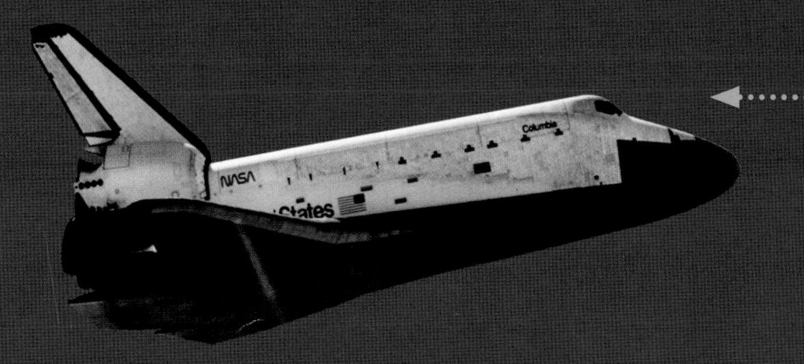

SPACE SHUTTLE COLUMBIA

The second was the space shuttle *Columbia*. Its mission was completed. But the shuttle exploded when it was returning to Earth. It happened on February 1, 2003. *Columbia* also had seven crew members. They all died.

FAMOUS

YURI GAGARIN

Yuri Gagarin was the first person to travel into space. He was Russian. His spacecraft was *Vostok 1*. He went into space on April 12, 1961.

ALAN SHEPARD

Alan Shepard was the first American to go into space. His spacecraft was *Freedom 7*. He went into space on May 5, 1961. He was also on the Apollo 14 mission. It went to the moon in 1971.

ASTRONAUTS

VALENTINA VLADIMIROVNA TERESHKOVA

Valentina Vladimirovna Tereshkova was the first woman in space. She was Russian. She went into space on June 16, 1963.

SALLY RIDE

Sally Ride was the first American woman in space. Her space flight was in 1983.

FAMOUS ASTRONAUTS

[CONTINUED]

NEIL ARMSTRONG

Neil Armstrong was the first person to walk on the moon. He was on the Apollo 11 mission. He first stepped onto the moon on July 20, 1969.

BUZZ ALDRIN

Buzz Aldrin was another Apollo 11 astronaut. He also walked on the moon.

DO YOU WANT TO BE AN ASTRONAUT?

It takes a lot of hard work to become an astronaut.
But it is one of the most exciting jobs you can have!

1. What is a trip into space called?

2. Why do things float around in space?

3. Astronauts never have time off when they are in space. ***True or false?***

THINK ABOUT IT!

Where in space would you want to go and why?

Answers 1. Mission or expedition 2. There is no gravity. 3. False

GLOSSARY

attach – to join or connect.

dangerous – able or likely to cause harm or injury.

degree – the unit used to measure temperature.

disaster – a sudden event that causes destruction and suffering or loss of life.

equipment – a set of tools or items used for a special purpose or activity.

filter – to clean a liquid by passing it through a device that removes any matter floating in it.

launch – to send a spacecraft or missile into space.

mattress – a large, thick pad that you sleep on.

pilot – a person who operates an aircraft or a ship.

plumbing – the pipes in a building that bring clean water in and carry dirty water out.

release – to set free or let out.